You And *All* Your House

How To Believe and Receive What God Has Provided

Brian McCallum

Brian McCallum Ministries
Broken Arrow, Oklahoma

Unless otherwise indicated, all scriptural quotations are from the *King James Version* of the Bible.

You And All *Your House: How To Believe and Receive What God Has Provided*
Published by:
Brian McCallum Ministries
12645 E. 127th St
Broken Arrow, OK 74011
ISBN 0-9620883-4-X

Editorial Consultant: Phyllis Mackall, Broken Arrow, Oklahoma

Cover design and book production by:
DB & Associates Design & Distribution
P.O. Box 52756, Tulsa, OK 74152

Printed in the United States of America.

Dedication

I want to dedicate this book to my wife, June, who has helped me to study these Scriptures, compile the Scriptures found in the Appendix, and, above all, to agree with me these many years as we prayed for our family.

I would further dedicate the book to those family members present and gone to be with the Lord whose lives were forever changed by the Lord as we prayed and stood in faith for them through Jesus Christ our Lord.

Contents

...he shewed us how he had seen an angel in his house, which stood and said unto him, Send men to Joppa, and call for Simon, whose surname is Peter;

Who shall tell thee words, whereby thou and all thy house shall be saved.

Acts 11:13,14

...Believe on the Lord Jesus Christ, and thou shalt be saved, and thy house.

Acts 16:31

Foreword

During one of the classes I teach at a Bible school, I recently asked a group of approximately 220 students to raise a hand if someone in their close family was either unsaved or backslidden.

I was surprised to see nearly every one raise a hand! The typical family of believers today appears to also include some non-believers or backslidden loved ones.

What does the Lord expect, and what has He provided for the believing ones to do to work His will in their families?

Jesus said to Peter in Luke 22:31,32, "...behold, Satan hath desired to have you, that he may sift you as wheat: But I have *prayed* for thee, that thy faith fail not: and when thou art converted, strengthen thy brethren."

From this example, we see God's will not only for Peter but for all mankind. We also see the enemy's desire to involve and hold mankind in works of darkness.

God would have all your family be converted, be strong in the Lord, and be able to strengthen others, including other members of your family.

This book will instruct us in the Word — the revealed will of God — and show us how to achieve the results Jesus was confident His prayer had provided for Peter: preservation, conversion (salvation), and strength to impart the Word to others.

I trust that the Spirit of Truth will guide you and witness of the truth in your heart as you read this book.

Brian K. McCallum

Broken Arrow, Oklahoma

January 1998

Chapter 1
Spiritual Life Begins

Proverbs 22:6 says, "Train up a child in the way he should go: and when he is old, he will not depart from it."

I have been a Christian for 33 years now, and in that time I have observed the fruit of that promise in many families that did train their children spiritually and naturally in the ways of God.

Faithfulness in children seems to be the direct result of faithfulness of parents to train their children in a godly manner and in God's ways. That is *the law of sowing and reaping* in action, producing predictable, biblical results.

I was 32 years old when I was born again and 37 before I came into the Full Gospel experience of the baptism in the Holy Spirit. It was also at that time that I came under the anointed teaching of the Word of God for the first time.

Soon I heard good teaching concerning Proverbs 22:6, and that truth became real to my understanding. But where did that leave me? My five children were mostly grown and still unsaved.

I had attended church since I was a child, but the denomination I belonged to was in great need of revival. To summarize that situation, in more than 30 years I never witnessed an altar call in that church!

We heard about God and His Son, Jesus, but no mention of a personal relationship was ever made. My children were raised in a Sunday School and church where no Gospel message was preached or taught.

I was saved watching Billy Graham preach on television. After that, I struggled in life, experienced divorce, and because of my military service during the Vietnam era, I saw far too little of my children in those years as they were growing up.

A Father's Place

It was 1970 when I finally saw the truth about my spiritual responsibility toward them. As revelation came, I began to take the scriptural place of a father to his children. At first, I tried mightily in my own strength to convince my son and four daughters that they needed to be saved. There was no outward result to all of this except with my youngest daughter.

I felt that perhaps I had missed my opportunity with my children, but God is good! He got my attention one day as I was reading from Acts 2:37-39:

> **Now when they heard this [the Gospel], they were pricked in their heart, and said unto Peter and to the rest of the apostles, Men and brethren, *What shall we do?***
>
> **Then Peter said unto them, Repent, and be baptized every one of you in the name of Jesus Christ for the remission of sins, and you shall receive the gift of the Holy Ghost.**
>
> **For the promise is unto you, *and to your children, and to all that are afar off,* even as many as the Lord our God shall call.**

I can tell you that what the Lord showed me that day was an enormous relief to me. It started the work of faith in me that led to my children's salvation and the work of faith in their lives.

An Act of Spiritual Authority

It was not only my children who were blessed. This work of grace encompassed my whole family, young and old alike. And it reached through my spiritual authority in days to come to many other children who came to the place of ministry in which the Lord placed me.

With such a late start in the walk of faith, how could this be? The verses we just read in Acts 2 hold the answer. With our trust in God's Word and the Spirit of Truth within, let us look steadfastly once again into the revelation of Jesus Christ and His great work of grace and mercy toward us, in us, and through us.

Chapter 2

And *All* Your House

Acts 2:37 tells us the first response of the people to whom Peter preached on the Day of Pentecost: "...Men and brethren, what shall we do?"

Eureka! They did *not* know what to do when they heard the truth, the Gospel of Jesus Christ. Why not? I thought I knew why, and I really related to those who had been saved later in life at the first Pentecostal outpouring in Jerusalem.

They were not like Simeon, Anna, and others who had looked for the Lord's redemption in Jerusalem (Luke 2:25,26,36-38).

In other words, those who were saved on the Day of Pentecost were not in covenant with God until that day! Yes, even though they had descended *naturally* from Abraham, they had not descended *spiritually* from him until they believed and received what Peter had preached about.

There was hope for me then, because Peter had said to *them,* "...Repent and be baptized...in the name of Jesus Christ for the remission of sins [I had already done this], and ye shall receive the gift of the Holy Ghost [and I had also received that]. For the promise is unto you, and to *your children....*"

Those words entered my heart, and I began to *know* they were meant for my children, too. But *how* would they receive the promise I myself had already received?

Again the Lord began to teach me the answer to that question. I use the word "began," because He hasn't stopped to this day. The light keeps getting brighter from faith to faith, glory to glory, and power to power.

God's Will for My Family

Sometime later He brought to my attention several passages of Scripture in John and Acts that showed me *how* it would come to pass and what God's will for my family was. Let us begin with John 4:46-53.

> **So Jesus came again into Cana of Galilee, where he made the water wine. And there was a certain nobleman, whose son was sick at Capernaum.**
>
> **When he heard that Jesus was come out of Judaea into Galilee, he went unto him, and besought him that he would come down, and heal his son: for he was at the point of death.**
>
> **Then said Jesus unto him, Except ye see signs and wonders, ye will not believe.**
>
> **The nobleman saith unto him, Sir, come down ere my child die.**
>
> **Jesus saith unto him, Go thy way; thy son liveth. And the man believed the word that Jesus had spoken unto him, and he went his way.**
>
> **And as he was now going down, his servants met him, and told him, saying, Thy son liveth.**
>
> **Then enquired he of them the hour when he began to amend. And they said unto him, Yesterday at the seventh hour the fever left him.**
>
> **So the father knew that it was at the same hour, in the which Jesus said unto him, Thy son liveth: and himself believed, and his whole house.**

Notice that when Jesus said to the nobleman, "Go thy way, thy son liveth," the man believed the word Jesus had spoken to him. He acted on it, and he went his way home. His servants met him on the way and told him his son was alive. The fever had left him the day before at the same hour Jesus had spoken to him and he had acted.

Household Salvation

This, in turn, produced another result: "...himself believed, *and his whole house.*" They must have heard from him what Jesus had said and what the man had done. Jesus' word, the man's obedience to it, and the miracle of healing brought life to his whole household. They *all* believed!

Now let us look at four similar examples in the Book of Acts. The first two are found in Acts 10 and 11.

> **There was a certain man in Caesarea called Cornelius, a centurion of the band called the Italian band.**
>
> **A devout man, and one that feared God with all his house, which gave much alms to the people, and prayed to God always.**
>
> **He saw in a vision evidently about the ninth hour of the day an angel of God coming in to him, and saying unto him, Cornelius.**
>
> **And when he looked on him, he was afraid, and said, What is it, Lord? And he said unto him, Thy prayers and thine alms are come up for a memorial before God.**
>
> **And now send men to Joppa, and call for one Simon, whose surname is Peter:**
>
> **He lodgeth with one Simon a tanner, whose house is by the sea side: he shall tell thee what thou oughtest to do.**

And when the angel which spake unto Cornelius was departed, he called two of his household servants, and a devout soldier of them that waited on him continually;

And when he had declared all these things unto them, he sent them to Joppa.

Acts 10:1-8

Cornelius was visited by an angel of God who told him how and where to find Peter, who, as Acts 11:14 says, "...shall tell thee words, whereby thou and *all thy house shall be saved."*

In Acts 10:44 we read, "While Peter yet spake these words, the Holy Ghost fell on all them which heard the word." There was the answer as to "how." *They would hear the Word and believe for themselves.* Do we see that anywhere else?

Lydia's Household Believes

We see another example in Acts 16:14,15. Lydia, a cloth merchant in the city of Thyatira, had her heart opened by God.

And a certain woman named Lydia, a seller of purple, of the city of Thyatira, which worshipped God, heard us: whose heart the Lord opened, that she attended unto the things which were spoken of Paul.

And when she was baptized, *and her household,* she besought us, saying, If ye have judged me to be faithful to the Lord, come into my house, and abide there. And she constrained us.

She "attended" to the things which Paul spoke. That means she received and acted on them. Then she and her household, who must have also heard and acted on Paul's Gospel message, were baptized. That indicates that salvation had come to her whole house.

The next testimony is of the Philippian jailer, also reported in Acts 16:

> **And at midnight Paul and Silas prayed, and sang praises unto God: and the prisoners heard them.**
>
> **And suddenly there was a great earthquake, so that the foundations of the prison were shaken: and immediately all the doors were opened, and every one's bands were loosed.**
>
> **And the keeper of the prison awaking out of his sleep, and seeing the prison doors open, he drew out his sword, and would have killed himself, supposing that the prisoners had been fled.**
>
> **But Paul cried with a loud voice, saying, Do thyself no harm: for we are all here.**
>
> **Then he called for a light, and sprang in, and came trembling, and fell down before Paul and Silas,**
>
> **And brought them out, and said, Sirs, what must I do to be saved?**
>
> **And they said, Believe on the Lord Jesus Christ, and *thou shalt be saved, and thy house.***
>
> **And they spake unto him the word of the Lord, and to *all that were in his house.***
>
> **And he took them the same hour of the night, and washed their stripes; and was baptized, *he and all his,* straightway.**
>
> **And when he had brought them into his house, he set meat before them, and rejoiced, *believing in God with all his house.***
>
> **Acts 16:25-34**

Here we also observe the Good News. Paul and Silas spoke the Word of the Lord to him, saying, "Believe on the Lord Jesus Christ, and thou shalt be saved, *and thy house.*" And the jailer and all who were in his household rejoiced, *believing in God.* They could do so because they had all *heard* the Word and *acted* on it.

In Acts 18, we see a similar testimony concerning Crispus, the chief ruler of the synagogue in Corinth.

> **And he...entered into a certain man's house, named Justus, one that worshipped God, whose house joined hard to the synagogue.**
>
> **And Crispus, the chief ruler of the synagogue, believed on the Lord *with all his house;* and many of the Corinthians hearing believed, and were baptized.**
>
> **Acts 18:7,8**

Crispus believed on the Lord with all his house when Paul preached in the house of Justus, next door to the synagogue. We also see how that came about in the eighth verse, "...and many of the Corinthians *hearing* believed, and were baptized."

We have now seen five examples where someone and *all* his or her house believed. That convinces me what the will of God is for my house. However, all the members of the family must hear the Word and believe it in order for God's will to be done in them.

Hearing the Truth

Since many families today are often spread out across our nation and even out of it, they don't necessarily have the opportunity to hear the Word together. That in no way diminishes the promise the Lord has made. It does, however, alter circumstances which often must be overcome for the promise to be fulfilled.

A process of overcoming must take place so family members can even hear the truth. Then another process of overcoming is usually necessary for those family members to enter wholeheartedly in service to the Lord.

Remember, if they had been trained up in the way they should go as children, the wholehearted part would already be present in their lives. This overcoming process takes time; sometimes many more years than we might like.

I recall being impatient with my own children's commitment and growth after they were saved. One day the Lord simply asked me, "How long did it take you to become wholehearted toward Me?"

"Oh, I see! You were long-suffering toward me, and You want me to be that way toward my children."

"Yes, son, you've got the idea."

Now we come to the first real work of love and faith we can do for our lost or backslidden family members — prayer.

Chapter 3

Praying With Confidence

It is important to remember that our first and sometimes greatest chance to show our love to lost or backslidden family members is to pray for them.

To pray with *confidence,* it is absolutely necessary to know what foundation we are standing on and, more specifically, what promises of God we are basing this faith on.

> **And this is the confidence that we have in him, that, if we ask any thing according to his will, he heareth us:**
>
> **And if we know that he hear us, whatsoever we ask, we know that we have the petition that we desired of him.**
>
> **1 John 5:14,15**

Asking according to God's revealed will — His Word — brings *confidence* that our prayers have been heard, and we now have as our present possession whatever we asked for. It is enlightening to see verse 16 in the same context:

> **If any man see his brother sin a sin which is not unto death, he shall ask, and he shall give him life for them that sin not unto death. There is a sin unto death: I do not say that he shall pray for it.**
>
> **1 John 5:16**

Believers can exert great influence in the lives of others by praying for them when they are burdened by sin, for example. This promise says that God will work in them because we ask. The person involved isn't praying for himself or herself at this point, so we need to exercise our covenant place in the Lord and ask on their behalf.

We can ask God to forgive them, and He will.

We can ask God to grant them repentance, and He will.

We can ask God to protect them during this time before they come to repentance, and He will.

And we can be confident that we have asked according to His will!

Old Testament Promises

Let us look at several promises in the Old Testament, remembering that every promise of God is yes and amen in Christ.

> **Thus says the Lord, "A voice is heard in Ramah, lamentation and bitter weeping. Rachel is weeping for her children; she refuses to be comforted for her children, because they are no more."**
>
> **Thus says the Lord, "Restrain your voice from weeping, and your eyes from tears; for your work shall be rewarded," declares the Lord, "And they shall return from the land of the enemy.**
>
> **"And there is hope for your future," declares the Lord. "And your children shall return to their own territory.**
>
> **"I have surely heard Ephraim grieving, 'Thou hast chastised me, and I was chastised, like an untrained calf; bring me back that I may be restored, for Thou art the Lord my God.**
>
> **"'For after I turned back, I repented; and after I was instructed, I smote on my thigh; I was ashamed,**

and also humiliated, because I bore the reproach of my youth.'

"Is Ephraim My dear son? Is he a delightful child? Indeed, as often as I have spoken against him, I certainly still remember him; therefore My heart yearns for him: I will surely have mercy on him," declares the Lord.

Jeremiah 31:15-20
New American Standard Bible

Here is a scriptural promise concerning the backslidden Israelites who were destined to be carried into captivity in Jeremiah's day.

Rachel symbolizes the believing remnant, distraught for her children who had gone into captivity because they had neither heeded the warnings nor repented of ungodliness in themselves.

God's Message of Hope

It is indeed a bitter pill to see your children or loved ones eating the fruit of their unrighteous ways. But look at what God said He would do for you in such a case. He said, "Restrain yourself from grief, for I can help you recover them."

A better way to see it is, you by faith and prayer can help God or give Him dominion in the lost or backslidden children to turn their hearts to Him. "*...Your work shall be rewarded,* declares the Lord." That is most definite. "And they shall return from the land [or influence] of the enemy. And there is hope for your future." What grace, what blessing to know this!

Notice that by saying that there is hope for the future, God is telling us that this will take time. Our role during this time is to hold on to the promise, no matter what we see or hear to the contrary. And we will see and hear natural facts that are contrary to what we are believing.

What specific biblical hope do we have? "Your children will return to their own territory" (or their covenant place in Christ).

For us today, that is much more than a geographical possession. It speaks to us of holiness, safety, prosperity of spirit, soul, and body, a godly lifestyle, and submission of heart and mind to the plan and purpose of God for their lives.

The place of repentance is seen in Ephraim's (backslidden Israel's) response to God, and the passage concludes with, "I will surely have mercy on him, declares the Lord" (verse 20). All this will happen because you didn't succumb to grief, but instead you did your work of faith and asked God in prayer on their behalf.

Deliverance for Captives

Now let's find another similar promise, this time in Isaiah 49:24,25.

> **Shall the prey be taken from the mighty, or the lawful captive delivered?**
>
> **But thus saith the Lord, Even the captives of the mighty shall be taken away, and the prey of the terrible shall be delivered: for I will contend with him that contendeth with thee, and I will save thy children.**

Those taken captive by Satan are lawful captives, we are told. But a believer can change that and bring deliverance to those in the devil's bondage. The captives of the mighty *shall be taken away,* and the prey of the terrible *shall be delivered,* this passage tells us.

Good news in the midst of a sad situation! Notice that when you do your work in covenant with

God, He will contend with the devil! Best of all, He *will* save (or deliver) your children.

One more witness to this is Second Chronicles 30:9.

> **For if ye turn again unto the Lord, your brethren and your children shall find compassion before them that lead them captive, so that they shall come again into this land: for the Lord your God is gracious and merciful, and will not turn away his face from you, if ye return unto him.**

Because you returned to God and did your work of faith, you have received compassion and mercy from Almighty God for your brethren and your children — all your house.

Chapter 4
Blessings Abound

When I surrendered my will to the will of God for my life and entered full-time ministry in 1973, the blessings of God began to multiply and increase by a large factor. Many of these blessings came to my own life, and many more occurred in the rest of my family.

It seemed to me at that time and in the months immediately following, answers to long-time prayers began to manifest. Things in my own personal life that had not come in line with God's plan and purpose now quickly lined up with the Word.

I still remember the discovery in my heart that I was called to teach God's Word. The anointing to do so greatly increased as I set my heart to follow God's will. It was true joy to finally be doing what the Lord had created me for. It still is.

My oldest child, Doug, related this story to me after the fact. In 1974, in this same time frame, his girlfriend asked him to take her to hear Billy Graham in Anaheim, California, near his home in Riverside.

Doug told me, "I didn't want to go, Dad, but she really wanted to, so I went. We sat high up in the stadium. It was as far from the ministry platform as I could get."

Remember, I was believing God that each of my children would receive Jesus as his or her Lord and Savior. I was decreeing God's salvation over them frequently.

Doug continued, "When Mr. Graham gave the altar call, it was as if I was catapulted out of my seat, and I found myself moving quickly toward the platform with the others who were responding to the altar call."

God's Faithfulness

There Doug gave his heart to Jesus and was born again. Later we had the privilege of working together in the ministry for a time. More about that later.

God is faithful! He watches over His Word to perform it, according to Jeremiah 1:12. A neighbor of my two oldest daughters invited them into her house for refreshments one hot summer day, and then led them to Jesus while they drank some lemonade! One by one, my children all committed their lives to Christ.

The Lord always does exceeding abundantly above what we have asked Him to. At this same time, I met my present wife, June. She came to work for the ministry I was engaged in, ministering to troubled teens. She was a committed Christian, which I saw from the first. She was the mother of four boys, the younger two still living in her single-parent home.

We began our life together as friends, praying and agreeing with each other that our children would believe God and receive His grace to be saved and serve Him wholeheartedly. The Lord graciously gave us a tender love for each other that developed and grew as we served the Lord together.

Praying for the Family

A little over 18 months later, we were married and are now living out God's promises together. As we are led by the Holy Spirit, we still pray together regularly for our whole family, which has now grown to include 21 grandchildren and one great-granddaughter.

We have faced many challenges to faith with or on behalf of our family, and one by one we have seen them overcome. This happened when we prayed and did what we could do for them in times of their need.

Our children all know the Lord and are all learning to serve Him from faith to faith and from glory to glory in their lives.

Finding the perfect will of God for our lives and walking in it brought blessings, answers to prayer, scriptural order, financial prosperity, and personal growth, not only to ourselves but to our whole house or family.

In our case, two families became as one, learned to love and care for each other, and have become truly one in the Lord. This salvation extended to our whole house and included older members of the family as well, as we shall see in the next chapter.

Chapter 5
Gray-Haired Grace

The promises we saw in John's Gospel and the Book of Acts were that different persons and their whole house believed. That had to have included the elder members of the family as well as the younger.

It does include them, and I would like to share how prayer for elder members of our own family bore fruit. Let me begin by noting that June's and my parents and their brothers and sisters in several cases were saved as children or young adults.

However, in every case they were either deluded or turned off by the churches they attended during the 1920s through the early 1970s.

These churches were infiltrated by liberalism and unbelief and had substituted man's doctrines for the Word of God. That is what our parents' generation either lived in or left behind for all those years.

When June and I began to pray for them, make supplication (definite requests) for them, intercede for them, and give thanks to God for their salvation, many answers began to appear.

I remember asking the Lord to help them receive grace and mercy. We asked God to give them repentance and a hunger and a thirst for righteousness. We asked the Lord to protect them and commissioned holy angels to encamp round about them to deliver them. We also asked the Lord to fill them with the Holy Spirit.

One day in the early 1980s, I was praying in our weekly staff prayer meeting at Rhema Bible Training Center, where I was teaching. Mrs. Lynette Hagin, the Director of Rhema, was leading that meeting.

After a time of prayer, she said she sensed in her heart that we should all pray for our family members who were lost or backslidden.

Praying for Older Relatives

I began to pray my usual prayers, as mentioned above, but soon I switched over to praying in other tongues. After about 30 minutes of this, I spoke these words out of my understanding: "Lord, I don't believe that You would let any of our older relatives leave this world in the spiritual condition they are now in!"

That was another way of my saying that I *firmly* believed that God had heard and answered our prayers for our elders' salvation and restoration in the truth.

The Lord has kept that word. All but five of the older family members have since died. They were all ready when they went, and they have some fruit of faithful works or reward in heaven. The Lord's mercies truly are from everlasting to everlasting.

> **But the lovingkindness of the Lord is from everlasting to everlasting on those who fear him. And His righteousness to children's children,**
>
> **To those who keep His covenant, and who remember His precepts to do them.**
>
> **Psalm 103:17,18 *NASB***

The two surviving elder members whom we are the closest to are June's father, aged 89, and my Aunt Mildred, aged 94. The others lived long lives. Most were more than 80 years old when they went to be with Jesus.

How Men Find God

Two anecdotes from Aunt Mildred's life are worth recounting here. When she was 85 and widowed, we visited her in Connecticut. Knowing that I was in the ministry, she asked me, "Brian, don't you think there are many ways that men can find God?"

I knew what she meant, because I, too, had heard that opinion expressed from the pulpit of our denominational church when I was younger. I felt an unction to say to her, "No, Aunt Mildred, I don't believe that, and here is why."

I picked up her Bible from the coffee table and read her what Jesus said in John 14:6, "...I am the way, the truth, and the life: *no man* cometh unto the Father, but by me." She was quiet for a minute or so.

Despite having prayed for her and being assured by the Lord that He was working in her, I trembled within as I waited for her response. She said, "Is that what the Bible says?"

I replied, "Yes, that is what the Word says." Without any more delay, she answered, "Well, that must be the way it is, then."

Glory to God, He is so good, so patient, and so merciful! Since that time she has asked us to pray for her, and we have on many occasions.

A Birthday Healing

Aunt Mildred turned 90 on May 28, 1993. We went to visit her and take her out to her favorite restaurant, The Under Mountain Inn in Lakeville, Connecticut.

June and I were shocked to see how stooped over she had become in the past year. Now she was no more than five feet tall, and she could hardly look up at us when she was seated at the table.

When we returned to her apartment in Salisbury, I told her the story of the woman with the spirit of infirmity in Luke 13:11-16, and asked if she would let us pray that the Lord would straighten her back to her normal 5 foot 8 height. After hearing the Bible story, she invited us to pray. We did, and left that day thanking God for her deliverance.

Three months later, Aunt Mildred fell in her apartment and broke a hip. We went to Connecticut again to help relocate her in a nursing home. We arrived at her room in the intermediate care section one morning. She'd had her hip pinned in the hospital and was already up walking with a four-point walker.

She looked different to us in her wing-backed chair, but we were a bit slow in grasping the reason for it. And we were surprised when she said, "Push my walker over here. I'll show you how to use it."

She continued, "You pull the walker up close, but don't lean on it getting to your feet. You lean on the chair getting to your feet, and then you take hold of the walker." She was a good pupil even at 90, willing to learn new things.

"Then you stand up to your full height with your hands on the walker," she said and proceeded to do so! I nearly fell out of my chair. She was standing perfectly straight!

We exclaimed, "Aunt Mildred, Aunt Mildred! You're straight, you're straight!"

"Oh yes," she replied. "I forgot to tell you."

God Shows Himself Merciful

How great is God's readiness and desire to show Himself merciful to the members of our families!

The Lord answered another prayer most abundantly for June's mother, "Lord, make the last years of her life better in every way than the beginning ones." This we had prayed for some time. At age 78, she had a severe stroke and heart attack. She was beyond all medical help in a coma. We were told she would die without regaining consciousness.

We prayed that the Lord would restore her to consciousness and health and that she could visit with all her family before she went to be with Him.

Almost overnight her condition dramatically improved to the point where she could be moved to a nursing home. June went to California to be with her, and all her immediate family members were with her for the next two weeks.

When June got there, her mother was up and walking around with help, but her mind was still not totally clear. She didn't recognize June. June's sister Royce noted that she was talking a lot, but Royce couldn't understand her. She told June, "It sounds like she is speaking another language."

A Restorative Miracle

June recognized that her mother was speaking fluently in another tongue, the spiritual gift of God! Soon afterwards, her mother's condition changed drastically.

She became clear headed and alert, which was a restorative miracle of God. As her family members visited day by day, she kept telling them how much she loved them. She even called me in Oklahoma and asked if she could come to visit! Then, after 30 days, she went to be with the Lord. God's mercies are new every morning!

> **It is of the Lord's mercies that we are not consumed, because his compassions fail not.**
>
> **They are new every morning: great is thy faithfulness.**
>
> **Lamentations 3:22,23**

Space does not allow me to tell of all the wonderful works of the Lord that happened in our elder relatives' lives in answer to prayer, but you can see how Almighty God responds when you take your full place in covenant relationship with Him.

Chapter 6
Love's Corresponding Actions

Praying for lost or backslidden family members is always the first and most timely action a believer can take. However, the Word and experience both tell us that prayer is not the last or only action to be taken in faith for such family members.

To begin looking into other corresponding actions of faith that demonstrate love for and to carnal and worldly family members, let us first consider the Scriptures.

> **And if I give all my possessions to feed the poor, and if I deliver my body to be burned, but do not have love, it profits me nothing.**
>
> **Love is patient, love is kind, and is not jealous; love does not brag and is not arrogant,**
>
> **does not act unbecomingly; it does not seek its own, is not provoked, does not take into account a wrong suffered,**
>
> **does not rejoice in unrighteousness, but rejoices with the truth;**
>
> **bears all things, believes all things, hopes all things, endures all things.**
>
> **Love never fails....**
>
> **1 Corinthians 13:3-8 *NASB***

Notice especially the fourth, fifth, seventh, and eighth verses: "Love is patient, love is kind...does not seek its own...does not take into account a wrong suffered...bears all things, believes all things, hopes all things, endures all things. Love never fails."

I will paraphrase these verses based on my experiences with my own family.

A Confession for Your Family

"I am patient with and kind toward my own family, acting from my heart toward them and showing acts of care and kindness when the opportunity comes to do so.

"I am more interested in their welfare than my own, even to investing myself, my substance, and my time when compassion of heart so leads me.

"I am not defeated by their wrong words or actions, nor do I take offense from them.

"I don't allow myself to magnify these wrongs, but I do magnify what the Word has promised me concerning those loved ones when wrong has been done by them.

"I receive strength from God in any negative circumstances so that I may continue to believe God's Word in that time of testing and trial.

"My hope stays strong in Christ, who is my hope, when evil or negative reports come.

"I endure and overcome when I am tempted to judge or think less of my loved ones because of their wrongdoings.

"I cannot fail to continue loving them, because the love of God is poured out in my heart, and that love — God's love in me by the Holy Spirit — cannot fail. (See Romans 5:5.) God cannot fail. Love does not fail to reach out to those in need."

United With the Love of God

Notice that this paraphrase of verses 4, 5, and 7 uses "I" and "my" in place of "love." This is a way of acknowledging that God's love is in me. It is like saying, "I am a love child, begotten in love by my Father God, who is love."

When I am making this as a confession of my faith in the paraphrased Scriptures, I think of how that effectively unites me with the love of God. That is exactly what happens when I agree in words from my heart with God's Word.

When love is strong in you and your actions, others will see and partake of that heavenly fruit. When they do, the seed of love is in it, and love will grow in them. Isn't that what we have been praying and believing for them to have and do?

What I have written as a paraphrase can be a strong confession of faith for you. Confession will bring or result in possession. Confession will lead you to love's action toward your loved one.

Discouragement and despair will try to come against you, but they will be driven away by the force of faith, hope, and love constraining you and guarding your mind, renewing it.

The Key To Winning the Lost

Now let me continue to share more of what is in my heart concerning how to win your unsaved or backslidden loved ones.

Love is inclusive, not exclusive. Never let a backslidden loved one think that you think less of him or her or want to avoid them. When your lost relative needs material help, be the first there with the most to offer.

Take any opportunity given to share wise counsel, but don't put them down with your words, and don't push your words at them. Be like Jesus dealing with the Laodicean Church.

> **Behold, I stand at the door and knock; if anyone hears My voice and opens the door, I will come in to him, and will dine with him, and he with Me.**
>
> **Revelation 3:20 *NASB***

What is a "knock"? First, it is not forced entry or kicking the door open.

Here is an example of knocking on the door of the carnal or lost person's heart.

You begin by asking the person, "Have you learned anything from this sad experience?"

They may reply, "No, and I don't care to," or words to that effect. That is not an open door. Do any act of mercy they will allow, but do not attempt any further instruction at that point.

Opening the Door to the Savior

Remember, Jesus said, "If any man open, I will come in." The person you are dealing with must open the door to you.

"What, then, is an open door in this example?"

They may reply, "I'm not sure what the lesson is, but I want to know." This person has now opened to Jesus and you, and He can now proceed to minister gently as you are led by His Spirit.

Do you see the difference? In both cases, your question was the "knock."

In the second case, the person who was questioned opened the door — their mind and heart — to further dialogue.

It is really simple, isn't it? In both cases you keep showing the practical application of love and care before and after the "knock."

Before too much time passes, knock on their door again if they didn't open it the first time. In the meantime, your continuing show of concern could have softened that heart.

Take the initiative — perhaps even in a letter — and wait for the door to open. Your prayers and faith for the person or persons involved will eventually result in the door being opened.

God at Work

We have had the experience of being isolated and separated from a beloved daughter for a very long time. We sent several "knocks" from afar over the years. Finally the door was opened, and reconciliation was made after 18 years.

Don't ever give up what you are believing, no matter what you hear or see! *God is working in them according to your faith in His Word.*

Now, every time we see or hear from this daughter, we are so thankful and glad we continued in faith concerning her. The Lord was so good to her and us over all those years of separation. You would not know today that any problem had ever occurred between us, because the past has been fully overcome in Christ.

Epistles Read of All Men

In summary, I want to go to a very clear passage of Scripture in Second Corinthians 3.

> **Ye are our epistle written in our hearts, known and read of all men:**

Forasmuch as ye are manifestly declared to be the epistle of Christ ministered by us, written not with ink, but with the Spirit of the living God; not in tables of stone, but in fleshy tables of the heart.

And such trust have we through Christ to Godward;

Not that we are sufficient of ourselves to think any thing as of ourselves; but our sufficiency is of God;

Who also hath made us able ministers of the new testament; not of the letter, but of the spirit: for the letter killeth, but the spirit giveth life.

2 Corinthians 3:2-6

This passage is amplifying the point that those of us who trust in Christ are an epistle...*known and read of all men,* written in our eternal spirit by the Spirit of God. The passage also conveys to us that this sometimes-silent witness is an able minister of the New Covenant in Christ — not of the letter of the Law, for that kills, but of the Holy Spirit, who gives life to us.

"You Shall Be Witnesses"

This agrees perfectly with what Jesus told His disciples as He was about to ascend into heaven.

But ye shall receive power, after that the Holy Ghost is come upon you: and ye shall be witnesses unto me both in Jerusalem, and in all Judaea, and in Samaria, and unto the uttermost part of the earth.

Acts 1:8

"...You shall receive power after that the Holy Ghost is come upon you: *and you shall be witnesses* unto me...." This says the Holy Spirit upon us will make us a witness.

Our whole life — our lifestyle and our actions — will be just as much a faithful, powerful witness of our Lord Jesus Christ as the words we speak.

In First Peter 3:1, we learn that an unbelieving husband can be won by the godly testimony — without teaching or preaching — of a wife who is in subjection to her husband according to God's Word.

Love Speaks Volumes

So you can see why you should not hide from unbelieving relatives. How are they going to read the epistle that you are if they don't see or hear from you much? Again, your love and care expressed in action, and your friendship and help in their times of trouble, will speak volumes to the heart of your child or other loved one who has strayed away from or never truly received God's truth.

Faith without works is dead, being alone, we read from James 2:14. Likewise, love without its corresponding actions or works is also dead, being just an idea that never received its means of expression.

Friends, you and I can and will give love its expression if we truly believe God's Word. It does take faith and hope to continue to walk in love. Be the person who through faith and patience with people inherits the promises!

Chapter 7
Our Spiritual Children

As I noted earlier, June and I met while working together in a ministry that was devoted to ministering the Gospel and grace to troubled teenagers 14 to 18 years old. The ministry was located in a large facility on 33 acres in Grass Valley, California.

Young people were referred to us from families, welfare workers, and probation departments. Over the years, we averaged 50 to 55 students enrolled at any given time in our Christian Academy and live-in training program.

Other aspects, such as vocational training, arts and crafts development, and work programs filled out the natural part of the program. However, the most important aspect, and the foundation of all else, was North Star Chapel and Pastor Bill Mansdoerfer's congregation of Bible-believing Christians who supported, helped, prayed, and made our spiritual witness real to these young people.

My job was director and associate pastor, which encompassed supervision of the staff, teaching, and much interaction with the student body from their arrival to their return to their homes. That was an open-ended period, depending on the young person's need and response to the Gospel.

June was our school nurse and often the cook for more than 80 persons. She, too, interacted with the students daily, as did most of our more than 25 staff members.

Another of my responsibilities was to organize and inspire prayer meetings and prayer "chains" to pray specifically for the ministry and the young people who were temporarily placed in our care.

At first I had an unsettled question as to how much authority we had in their lives, since we were in a position of ministry and supervision over them for a relatively short period.

The Authority of the Great Commission

As I sought the Lord about this, He gave me insight by the light of His Word. First, He showed me Matthew 28:18-20.

> **And Jesus came and spake unto them, saying, All power is given unto me in heaven and in earth.**
>
> **Go ye therefore and teach all nations, baptizing them in the name of the Father, and of the Son, and of the Holy Ghost.**
>
> **Teaching them to observe all things whatsoever I have commanded you: and, lo, I am with you always, even unto the end of the world.**

I recognized that this Great Commission, as we refer to it, gave me authority in my calling and place of responsibility in ministry much like the place God had ordained in my own family. He also spoke to me through First Peter 5:1-4.

> **The elders which are among you I exhort, who am also an elder, and a witness of the sufferings of Christ, and also a partaker of the glory that shall be revealed:**

Feed the flock of God which is among you, taking the oversight thereof, not by constraint, but willingly; not for filthy lucre, but of a ready mind;

Neither as being lords over God's heritage, but being ensamples to the flock.

And when the chief Shepherd shall appear, ye shall receive a crown of glory that fadeth not away.

We also need to note verses 2 and 3 from the *NASB* version:

shepherd the flock of God among you, exercising oversight not under compulsion, but voluntarily, according to the will of God; and not for sordid gain, but with eagerness;

nor yet as lording it over those allotted to your charge, but proving to be examples to the flock.

Being a Shepherd to the Flock

Notice that we are charged by God to feed or shepherd (supply the spiritual need of) the flock among us, and that we should do this for those "allotted to our charge," as the *NASB* translation puts it.

What more authority to pray do we need for those the Lord leads us to or those He brings to us for help?

Our prayers for these young people became charged with faith, and 75 to 80 percent of the young people we took in were saved while they were with us!

Others testified that they received Jesus as Lord and Savior after they left because of the seed that had been planted firmly in their hearts while they were students at North Star Ministries.

During this time, my son, Doug, came to visit and then to stay. He worked with us for more than a year and then married Karol, a fellow staff member, before they left to pursue their lives together in Christ.

That was a precious time for me to see how the Lord blessed and used him.

Prayers That Avail Much

It pays great dividends to pray as James 5:16 *(The Amplified Bible)* relates.

> **Confess to one another therefore your faults — your slips, your false steps, your offenses, your sins; and pray** [also] **for one another, that you may be healed and restored — to a spiritual tone of mind and heart. The earnest (heartfelt, continued) prayer of a righteous man makes tremendous power available — dynamic in its working.**

Our prayers had availed much for other people's children, and our own children's blessings also increased as we prayed. The law of sowing and reaping was at work.

Chapter 8
Eternal Blessing

More than 24 years of full-time ministry and four years of part-time work for the Lord before that have put me in contact with people who have suffered deep grief over the untimely loss of a family member.

For some, nagging doubts as to the spiritual condition of their loved one perpetuated their grief long beyond the time that God's comfort would have relieved and ended it.

In ministering to such persons, I was always led to take them back to what they had believed for their loved one while they were living. In almost every case, believing prayer had been made in some way that they would yield to God, repent, return, or receive salvation in Christ.

My leading was to assure those left behind that the Spirit of Grace and Truth had ministered to their loved one through someone, because a believer's prayer has to be answered, as we see in the following Scriptures.

And this is the confidence that we have in him, that, if we ask any thing according to his will, he heareth us:

And if we know that he hear us, whatsoever we ask, we know that we have the petition that we desired of him.

If any man see his brother sin a sin which is not unto death, he shall ask, and he shall give him life for them that sin not unto death. There is a sin unto death: I do not say that he shall pray for it.

1 John 5:14-16

For the promise is unto you, and to your children, and to all that are afar off, even as many as the Lord our God shall call.

Acts 2:39

Sometimes the grieving relatives who had believed were aware of the answer in various manifestations, and sometimes they were not. In my own case, three of my children were saved for more than a year before I knew about it!

A Revelation From the Book of Job

There was another principle or doctrine of God which He revealed to me as I read the Book of Job in years past. That doctrine is outlined in these Scriptures:

There was a man in the land of Uz, whose name was Job, and that man was blameless, upright, fearing God, and turning away from evil.

And seven sons and three daughters were born to him.

His possessions also were 7,000 sheep, 3,000 camels, 500 yoke of oxen, 500 female donkeys, and very many servants; and that man was the greatest of all the men of the east.

And his sons used to go and hold a feast in the house of each one on his day, and they would send and invite their three sisters to eat and drink with them.

And it came about, when the days of feasting had completed their cycle, that Job would send and consecrate them, rising up early in the morning and offering burnt offerings according to the number of them all; for Job said, "Perhaps my sons have sinned and cursed God in their hearts." Thus Job did continually...

Now it happened on the day when his sons and his daughters were eating and drinking wine in their oldest brother's house,

that a messenger came to Job and said, "The oxen were plowing and the donkeys feeding beside them,

and the Sabeans attacked and took them. They also slew the servants with the edge of the sword, and I alone have escaped to tell you."

While he was still speaking, another also came and said, "The fire of God fell from heaven and burned up the sheep and the servants and consumed them, and I alone have escaped to tell you."

While he was still speaking, another also came and said, "The Chaldeans formed three bands and made a raid on the camels and took them and slew the servants with the edge of the sword; and I alone have escaped to tell you."

While he was still speaking, another also came and said, "Your sons and your daughters were eating and drinking wine in their oldest brother's house,

and behold, a great wind came from across the wilderness and struck the four corners of the house, and it fell on the young people and they died; and I alone have escaped to tell you."

Then Job arose and tore his robe and shaved his head, and he fell to the ground and worshiped.

And he said, "Naked I came from my mother's womb, and naked I shall return there. The Lord gave and the Lord has taken away. Blessed be the name of the Lord."

Through all this Job did not sin nor did he blame God.

Job 1:1-5,13-22 *NASB*

And the Lord restored the fortunes of Job when he prayed for his friends, and the Lord increased all that Job had twofold.

Then all his brothers, and all his sisters, and all who had known him before, came to him, and they ate bread with him in his house; and they consoled him and comforted him for all the evil that the Lord had brought on him. And each one gave him one piece of money, and each a ring of gold.

And the Lord blessed the latter days of Job more than his beginning, and he had 14,000 sheep, and 6,000 camels, and 1,000 yoke of oxen, and 1,000 female donkeys.

And he had seven sons and three daughters.

And he named the first Jemimah, and the second Keziah, and the third Keren-happuch.

And in all the land no women were found so fair as Job's daughters; and their father gave them inheritance among their brothers.

And after this Job lived 140 years, and saw his sons, and his grandsons, four generations.

And Job died, an old man and full of days.

Job 42:10-17 *NASB*

Summarizing the Principle

Four points serve to summarize this principle:

First, Job was an upright or righteous man, which means he was in covenant relationship with the living God, who had granted Him right standing because of His faith. (See also Job 19:25-27.)

Second, Job continually made believing covenant sacrifices (a form of prayer) for the children he had — all of them.

Third, Job's children died prematurely. Their natural lives ended too soon, which was very grievous to him.

Fourth, God did restore the fortunes of Job when he prayed for his friends, and the Lord increased *all t*hat Job had *twofold.*

When I read Job 42:12, I saw that God had given a twofold increase to Job in sheep, camels, oxen, and donkeys. After Job's fortunes were restored, there were twice as many of each kind of animal as Job had lost.

The Twofold Blessing

However, when I read Job 42:13,14, it seemed that Job had only 10 more children, not 20 more, as the twofold blessing would seem to require at first glance.

> **And he had seven sons and three daughters.**
>
> **And he named the first Jemimah, and the second Keziah, and the third Keren-happuch.**
>
> **Job 42:13,14 *NASB***

I asked the Lord, "Why didn't You double the number of Job's children?"

His answer was, "I *did!*" Then, very gently He explained that sheep, camels, oxen, and donkeys were animals, not eternal beings, but sons and daughters were eternal!

Because of his faith and their faith in a covenant-keeping God, Job's first seven sons and three daughters were not lost eternally; only in this life.

So the eternal truth is that Job had 20 children in all — 14 sons and six daughters! He still does, and since their lives on Earth all eventually ended, Job lives in glory with all 20 of his children. The Lord *did* double or give Job twofold in children!

This truth helps to see things from God's view and to walk by faith in the revelation He gives.

Deliverance From Grief

There have been many men and women who came to me carrying a burden of grief long past its time but left with a smile and a gleam in their eye after hearing and receiving this truth.

I know full well the blessing that I speak of from my own bitter experience. Doug, my firstborn son, changed his life's direction as a young man of 23 and learned to fly to fulfill his heart's desire to become a missionary pilot.

He did everything right, first attending Spartan School of Aeronautics in Tulsa for 18 months and graduating with single- and multi-engine pilot ratings as well as commercial, instrument, and instructor ratings.

Being an experienced pilot myself, I flew with him several times in those 18 months. He demonstrated well-developed, well-balanced pilot skills for one so young in aviation.

I felt he was ready for the next step, an income-producing job that would allow him to accumulate flying time and experience quickly. The organization he expected to join for missionary work required that he have 1,500 flying hours in various types of aircraft.

Doug found a job in Northern California at a small town airport near Santa Rosa. He moved his family, now grown to include two daughters, to that area and went to work as an instructor pilot for a Piper aircraft dealer at that field.

Tragedy Strikes

All went well for five months. Then, in mid-November 1980, our daughter-in-law, Karol, called us late at night in Oklahoma to tell us that Doug and his student had been killed in a crash at the Santa Rosa Airport during an instructional flight.

It happened to be her birthday, and she and her parents were waiting to celebrate the event at their home when the news arrived. We were all completely shocked and greatly grieved. That is not something you expect to happen to a believer who was following God's will.

The comfort and help of the Holy Spirit in the next few weeks was so great and supernatural, it helped all of us overcome and do what had to be done. More importantly, His help allowed us to make right decisions that would affect Karol and their daughters, Elise and Erin, for many years to come.

In hindsight, I can say that we did make the correct decisions then, and God has blessed all of them in many ways over these last 17 years. It was eight or nine years before I saw the revelation I just related to you from the Book of Job.

God's Comfort Brings Closure

Again, God's comfort at the time of loss and since was great for the whole family. June's four sons have been like sons to me in all the years since, and I have also known many fine young men at Rhema Bible Training Center. However, when I saw the revelation I described to you from the Book of Job, there was a real closure in my heart about my son's untimely death, even though I no longer felt continual loss.

Now I feel a great anticipation of the eternal truth which I rejoice in as I go about my life's work in this world. God is *so* good to me! He does comfort us completely in all our tribulation.

Doug and I and all our family will rejoice in full union in Christ for all eternity! Whatever is lost temporally in this world is not nearly so important as the eternal blessing will be.

Chapter 9
Call to Action

What should you do with the knowledge you have acquired from this book?

If you take no action following or corresponding to the scriptural truths you have looked into, there will not be any positive change in the spiritual condition or circumstances of your relatives' lives.

To me, this seems to be like the proverbial women's work, which is "never done." Jesus said in Luke 18:1, "...men ought always to pray, and not to faint."

I could have filled this book with "horror stories" concerning some of our children and other family members. Over the years since I learned how to pray for my family, evil reports or observed actions often came to our attention.

The reason I did not include those accounts is simple. It is God who must be glorified and magnified; not things contrary to Him and certainly not what Satan does when he is given a place to work.

June and I are still learning how to stand strong, and having done all (in faith) to stand continually, despite what we see or hear to the contrary. Through our faith, the Word of God will grow mightily and prevail over circumstances and fleshly works in our loved ones.

In praying, making supplications, intercessions, and giving of thanks, we need to be consistent in meeting challenges which are presented to us by observed circumstances, evil reports, and sometimes by leadings of the Holy Spirit.

Some situations involving our family members will take longer to come to the full manifestation of victory we long to see in them. We must take our stand solidly on the Word of God, continue to give thanks for the answers we have believed and received, and never give in to our emotional self, which can swing wildly when circumstances and evil reports present themselves.

I would not change my mind about what I am believing for any family member, no matter what I observed or what I heard about him or her. To do that, we must continually keep the scriptural truth before our eyes and ears and keep it in the midst of our heart. Thank God, He is faithful even when we might be faithless.

If you see that you have spoken or acted faithlessly concerning your loved ones, repent quickly, return to God's grace for your comfort and strength, and go on in faith and prayer, believing for God's best for them.

If Your Feelings Betray You

It is not our mortal humanity that believes; it is the eternal spirit man who must arise and take control of our humanity in such circumstances.

So don't be surprised or dismayed should your feelings betray you at times. Mine have, but I have learned to put those failed feelings aside consciously and feed my spirit man the food he loves in even greater measure.

In the Appendix that follows you will find a list of "Faith for Family" food you can use frequently to keep yourself on track and your biblical hope strong in the will of God.

May the Lord richly bless you as you demonstrate His love by your believing prayer for your family.

Appendix

The Seed of the Righteous

There are precious and specific promises in the Word of God regarding the seed of the righteous. The terms "the seed of the righteous," "children," and other general references to our offspring can be applied to our natural children, our spiritual children, our whole family, and those over whom we have even temporary responsibility.

Prayer is one way we take responsibility for the above categories. In our dealings with the lost or the backslidden, prayer is the most effectual and essential element in manifesting our love toward them.

To pray for lost or backslidden children or family members, one must have confidence that he is doing so in agreement with God's will. This confidence can only be founded on God's revealed will, His Word.

Therefore, June and I have compiled this list of Scripture references from both the Old and New Testaments. Some are explained in this book. Others are left for your own study and application in your life. Strong faith and strong biblical hope come from knowing God's Word.

When studied and acted upon, these Scriptures will provide the necessary foundation for your stand on behalf of unsaved or backslidden loved ones.

Romans 15:4 states, "For whatsoever things were written aforetime were written for our learning, that we through patience and comfort of the scriptures might have hope."

Second Corinthians 1:20 agrees: "For *all* the promises of God in him are yea, and in him Amen, unto the glory of God by us."

When this foundation becomes more real to you than any other source of information, you are truly standing on your foundation. Then you will have good success!

New Testament Scriptures

John 14:12-15	John 4:43-53
John 15:7-17	Acts 2:16-21
1 John 3:21-24	Acts 2:38,39
1 John 5:14,15	Acts 10:1-8,44
Matthew 15:21-42	Acts 11:11-14
Mark 5:21-42	Acts 16:14,15
Mark 9:23	Acts 16:25-34
Luke 7:11-17	Acts 18:7,8

Old Testament Scriptures

Genesis 17:1-22	Psalm 127:1-5
Deuteronomy 7:9-15	Psalm 128:1-6
Deuteronomy 28:1-4	Proverbs 11:21
Deuteronomy 30:6-20	Proverbs 12:7
2 Chronicles 30:9	Proverbs 14:26
Psalm 25:12-14	Proverbs 20:7
Psalm 27:10	Isaiah 49:24-26
Psalm 37:25,26	Isaiah 54:10-13
Psalm 78:1-8	Isaiah 59:20,21

Psalm 89:24-36
Psalm 102:25-28
Psalm 103:8-18
Psalm 112:1-3
Isaiah 61:8,9
Isaiah 65:23
Jeremiah 31:15-20

"Having Done All, To Stand"

"For with the heart man believeth unto righteousness *[which is the written promise]*; and with the mouth confession is made unto salvation" *[which is the manifestation of the written promise]* (Romans 10:10).

The promise *in the Word is my written guarantee* that I have what I asked for even before it is manifested.

"Thou wilt keep him in perfect peace *[all is well for the one]*, whose thinking is molded and *stayed on the Word"* (Isaiah 26:3 paraphrased).

Heart faith *stays on the Word:* head faith strays from the Word.

"In conclusion, be strong in the Lord — be *empowered* through your union with Him; draw your strength from Him — that strength which His [boundless] might provides" *[in His Word]* (Ephesians 6:10 *Amp).*

Books by Brian K. McCallum

The Day of the Lord
Breaking the Bread of Revelation
Seven Letters to Seven Churches
Israel: God's Glory
Ministering Spirits Sent Forth

To Contact Brian K. McCallum
for speaking engagements
or to order books, please write:

Brian McCallum Ministries
12645 E 127th St
Broken Arrow, OK 74011